Light Filling My Bones

Light Filling My Bones

Poems by
Dorothy B. Anderson

Illustrations by
Donna Bruhl

HOBBLEBUSH BOOKS

ISBN 13: 978-0-9760896-4-3
ISBN 10: 0-9760896-4-5
Library of Congress Control Number: 2006921116

Designed and composed at Hobblebush Books, Brookline, New Hampshire

Text and display are Fournier MT, with poems set 11.3/14. In 1924, Monotype based this face on types cut by Pierre Simon Fournier circa 1742 and called "St. Augustin Ordinaire" in Fournier's *Manuel Typographique*. These types were among the earliest of the "transitional" style of typeface.

The cover and interior illustrations are cut-paper collages by Donna Bruhl.

Printed in China

Published by:

Hobblebush Books

17-A Old Milford Road
Brookline, New Hampshire 03033

www.hobblebush.com

ACKNOWLEDGMENTS

Grateful acknowledgments to the journals where some of the poems have appeared in earlier versions:

"Gloves," *Yankee Magazine*

"Lilacs," *Comstock Review*

"Taking Turns," *Potato Eyes*

"Ikebana Artist," *Victory Park*

"Amah," *Worcester Review*

"Mechanic Arts High School 1950," *Creative Juices*

"Heirloom," *Flashpoint*

"Pilot Light," "At Last," *National Library of Poetry*

"Pearls," *Diner*

"Sugaring," *Pine Island Journal*

"Mentor," "Sister," *Edison Review*

"Another Language," Poetry Society of New Hampshire

"At the Airport Restaurant," *Edison Literary Review*

Some of the poems appeared in the chapbook, *By the Yangtze*, published by Pudding House Publications.

Special thanks to my brother Martin Bruhl, who encouraged me to publish my poems. My sister-in-law Marcia Galloway was a great help when I first started, and my husband Paul and my son David were a real support.

Thanks to Sid Hall, poet and publisher, for his suggestions and for designing this book.

I would not have gotten anywhere without the assistance of friend and mentor, New Hampshire Poet Laureate Patricia Fargnoli, who edited the manuscript and made many good suggestions. Also thanks go to my poet friends, Susan Roney-O'Brien, Linda Warren, and Juli Nunlist, who know these poems well.

For my family, and husband Paul

CONTENTS

I

II

III

Light Filling My Bones

Moving on or going back to where you came from . . .

—Amy Clampitt
"A Procession at Candlemas"

✦ THE BATH

A wooden tub sits on the kitchen floor,
a whiff of onion alters to soap-perfume,
Amah pours kettles of steaming water
for our weekly bath.

The kitchen door is fastened with a hook.
Brother, cook, Dad, banished,
Amah allows only my younger sister
into our cleansing ritual.

One toe in, then all of me
froglike, curled in six inches
of precious water,
sliding into the scented warmth,
as Amah crouches beside me,
trickles water down my back,
lifts my braids.
Her long nails scrub my scalp,
she rains water on my head.

She washes my back and praises
my emerging waistline.
"Daughter Number One,
I see breasts like waterlily pods,"
I ask if that is good.
"The best" she smiles.
I wash my breasts, thighs,
newly-haired genitals with careful pride
as she rinses affection over me,
then stands and turns
to my little sister
impatiently waiting on her towel.
"Daughter Number Two
your turn is coming."

✦ Amah Curses Fate

Early that morning I could not find you.
Cook was strange when I asked for you.
Beyond the courtyard wall I heard a piercing wail.
"What's wrong with Amah?"
Cook stared at the pan of roiling oil.
"She's angry at her son."
"Is she scolding him?"
"No, her heart is sick and she must heal it."
I ran outside the courtyard gate to find you.
You stood alone, a circle of others around you.
Hair unoiled, uncombed, clothes shredded, shoes ripped,
fists shaking to the sky.
Aya—the veins on your neck pushed out peal after peal after peal—*Aya*
down the streets—*Aya*
over the wall—*Aya*
"I curse the Wind, I curse the Heavens—Aya
I curse the mother who bore you,
the father who spawned you.
Damn the womb which gave you life—Aya
You have disgraced your roots and trampled on them—Aya—Aya"

Where did my gentle Amah go?
That night after supper, oiled and combed, hoarse,
you readied me for bed.
I did not dare ask.
Your mouth was tight and locked—*Aya*.

✦ On My Way to School

The bearded Sikh, red-turbaned,
stands a fierce guard at the jewelry store.
I cross the street to Bombko's bakery
to wheedle lollipops for lunch,
then dash past the stamp store and
meet Alex at the end of the block.

We run beyond the Chinese school
where children are singing
in high-pitched voices,
past the Russian church, where
the robed priest waves from the yard.
Race the long no-stores block
to St. Mary's oaken door.

Only then do we stop,
lean against damp walls, laugh.
We've beaten them again, the Spanish kids
coming round the corner,
Victor, Jaime, Tonino —
We tie our shoelaces,
straighten our starched blue uniforms.
Alex giggles,
whispers a Chinese swear word.
I pinch him.
"Good morning, Mother Cecilia,"
I curtsy as the brown-frocked nun scurries past.

✴ Mechanic Arts High School 1950

Our English teacher, in front of the class,
book in one hand,
waved the other as she
recited Shakespeare in a deep voice.
Humid August, jammed desks,
as my fellow classmates stretched, yawned,
she strode and turned full face —
A teacher actor —
Words like jewels fell out of a velvet sack
onto the classroom floor.

She stopped.
When she stopped, we begged her to go on,
in that old high school years ago.
I don't remember her name - -
but she set a torch to dry words,
painted speaking in iridescent blues,
greens, reds and gold.

✦ HEIRLOOM

Oma's dusting-sugar spoon,
delicate curved arm,
a silver half-moon with holes,
rested in the sugar bowl in Hankow, China.

"Give me a tea spoon that
does not spill!" my father roared
eating his porridge.
He used his cereal spoon to ladle sugar,
shook his head in disgust.

Growing up in China,
we children loved the trail
of sugar grains it made.
We licked our fingers, pressed
them into the sweet hail as
we fought to use Oma's spoon.

Fifty years later it sits
on lumpy brown sugar,
in a green ceramic bowl,
admired by all my guests,
like an empress on her throne.

✴ WAR SCARS

Nights in China when I was nine,
escaping Japanese bombs,
Dad led with flashlight
to the basement.
Holding my plastic doll
under my raincoat,
I followed my younger sister
with our leashed dachshund.
Mother carried baby Martin.
We sat on the edge of our cots,
heard the constant hum of planes —
sometimes a siren.

On the news tonight,
a gap-toothed nine year old,
holds a thermos under one arm,
a copper kettle in the other . . .
His family flees Kabul
at night for fear of planes.

I know what's behind that grin.
When he pours water
from the kettle — does it
hold the grit of sand?
Does it cling to his hair,
creep into his pants? —
We both feel it dig into the
raw soles of our feet —
Fear stays — stays — stays —

✳ A Picture from China

This is the last photograph.
I take it everywhere.
It blots out the gray
of her face in the hospital bed.
She is standing
on the clinic terrace
in her white doctor's coat, smiling.
Behind her in the distance
are the spires and rooftops of Hankow.

She asked for me before she died;
"I made a mistake," she said,
I will never get well,"
"Mama you must be well,"
I cried, clasping her hand.
In the hospital we children saw her
sleeping before we went to bed.
She died that night. We were
not allowed to attend the funeral.

At first Father thought she fell,
and Grandma believed
it had to be an accident.
The Japanese had taken
the stairwell rails to fuel the war.
We lived on the third floor
but our servants found
her watch and rings
in a neat row by the elevator
opening on the fourth floor.

✦ ESCAPE

After Mother's death,
I stopped feeling warm.
We'd fled Hankow by boat downriver,
war erupting as we left,
a wooden sampan, sails and matting roof, our home.
We curled like knotted yarn under that roof.
The boatmen sailed for many days—

Father talked—he seldom talked before—
of freedom from possessions,
of being safe, of hope.
I wrapped blankets around me.

Grandmother cried—she always cried—
She told us of mother as a child
clowning on stilts.
Once docked, the dog escaped her rope.
The boatmen left without her.
Screaming, we begged to turn around.
We found her on the river's edge,
muddied fur, torn paws.
Always I was cold.

Men with guns stopped us,
then let us go.
"Bandits," our father said.
Then Huangchow—
a Swedish Christmas, candles,
homebaked *lefse*—and singing.
Warmth slid over me
like rain.

✦ DECEMBER 8TH, 1944

It always seems to snow this day.
Snow blows over meadows
as I walk,
ruts dusted white
as they were when she died.
In my family
I am the carrier of numbers.
Natal days, saint's days, death days.
The date of mother's suicide is heavy.
I feel harnessed to it
like a water carrier
shouldering buckets.

I wrap my coat around me
against the chilly air,
feel fifty-one years of imprint
in the tissues of my cells.

No other one,
not even my brother,
remembers the date.
I will carry it
with me when I die.
The date of mother's suicide
in China, will be buried
with me in a land
that was never her home.

✴ PIANO MUSIC IS BREAD FOR THE SOUL

for Oma

Her Steinway followed her
from Germany to China.
Shipped and crated, it stood deep in
water in a Shanghai warehouse.
One day it appeared, safe and melodious.
Oma, weeping and stroking it,
let me touch the keys.

I see her hand gliding over keys,
her arms swaying
as she builds crescendos
into sudden crests of sound.
Her eyes riveted, fingers flying,
at her grand piano, Oma,
my grandmother.

I learned to read music turning pages
for trio evenings in China,
Oma at the piano conducting,
cuffing my head if I missed a cue.
After we came to America
lives of composers lined her shelves,
dropped notes clung to ceiling, to walls,
danced across her piano lid.

I remember the lessons.
"Don't flatten the keys," she'd say,
showing me how to hold my fingers.
"Are you practicing?" she'd ask.

✦ ELEGY

for Singer Jan DeGaetani

Sometimes I hear you humming
when I cook soup.
Leftovers, chicken, peppers,
a sprig of rosemary.
I feel your hand on my arm
as you dip a finger in
It needs more salt.

Remember that summer
on Shell Beach, on Shelter Island
when I told you I was pregnant?
You burst into song,
yodels and clapping
as we entered the ocean
to frolic and splash.

Twenty-eight years of sharing
tears and jokes,
weddings, children,
concerts and tributes.
With music you expanded joy
consoled grief with song.

Sometimes you come to me
in dreams—
a doe's footprint in snow.

✦ At the Airport Restaurant

Restaurant fluorescent lights buzz above us.
Don sits across from me, his hand on my arm.
I know what he is going to say
and I do not want to hear it.

I know what I am going to say
but cannot say it yet.
I remember the pies I baked for him —
apple, and plum tarts.

His blue shirt is familiar,
I gave it to him last Christmas.
Right now I have trouble hearing him speak.
When afraid, I cannot listen.

He's telling me that our marriage is over.
He knows that I know it.
I love the hair on his arms and stare at it.
I cannot look at his eyes.

✴ MENTOR

for Mathilde McKinney

She sits at the piano in her room
in the retirement home.
Her gnarled fingers draw clear phrasing
of Debussy's Etude #5 from the keys.

At seventy, she retired
to the New Hampshire mountains,
played the antique organ in church,
taught my six-year-old son
how to place his fingers
and compose jazz.

After my husband left, she became my guide.
Her refrain:
"Solitude is a challenge, use it!"
My piano tuned, I began to practice
to rediscover Bach preludes.

Now at ninety-three,
she completes the etude,
looks at me, smiles,
"I'm out of practice."

✴ EXPLAINING TO MY SON

Your grandmother would go to the piano
in our home in China and play Mendelsohn,
her blonde hair falling
over her cheeks, sigh,
and sing German children's songs,

Some days she worried that Hitler
would win and rule.
She was only thirty-six
when she leapt to her death
in an elevator shaft during the war

When I was thirty-six,
you were conceived.
I'd practice Bach Inventions —
My pregnancy sprouted wings,
joyful notes and phrases.

Today your nimble fingers
herald our New Year's celebration
on the piano. Jazz fugues
flying from the keys —

✴ THE PILOT LIGHT

for Bill Matthews

You are staying with us again,
while teaching at the Frost Place.
I am with you in the kitchen
of my Franconia house,
telling you how I love your poems.

You smell of beer.
Your cigarette hangs from your mouth
as you speak nonstop,
choosing phrases in concentrated
elipses of clarity—
rings around a milky
moon at night.

"Death flickering in you
like a pilot light" speaks to me
of making most of time
before it outruns you,
like the walk we took at the Flume
to watch the river foam over boulders
grinding pebbles into sand.

I can't believe that you are gone—

✦ IKEBANA ARTIST

The greyhaired Japanese woman
in a strict folded kimono,
sits on a stool at the Keene street fair.

She builds a canvas with curving vines.
Three full-lipped golden lily blossoms
around one closed-eyed bud,
a shift of stem length,
a break of branch, a pull of flower leaf.

Spare movements of hands,
fingers slowly balancing.
We watch.

She stops.
Someone claps—she bows.
Begins again.

✦ BONSAI

Curled silently into itself, the peppermint tea tree
finds our table top its oasis.
Tiny white flowers
shine among the moss-green leaves.

Nervous, I immerse it
twice a week, allow water to swell
over the velvet moss to the twisted trunk
and wait for the water to stop bubbling.

The shape of the tree is like my
own peculiar bends and kinks,
my persistence in carving out
fate's eternal twists.

✦ MUSICAL MEMORY

For Don Anderson (1931–1991)

At the string dealer's cluttered shop,
when you first played the instrument,
we were told that it was a Guarnerius
built by the Cremona master in 1796.
Your adoration for it exploded.
I need this cello,
I won't eat or sleep until I have it.
We borrowed, we bought it.

Your hands and fingers
melded with the ebony fingerboard.
The cello sang your motifs,
its liquid notes bent to your muse.
It became your solace —
your companion.

Even today, when I hear a cello sonata,
I see your right hand guiding the bow.
The long fingers of your left
stretch and slide over
auburn polished wood
as a baritone resonance rises
into the stratosphere.

✦ FOR DAVID

I see you in Dad's tux—
shoulders broad, expansive chest
as you breathe in musical rhythm.
Musician's son,
you breathe like a metronome.

Your long-fingered hands are his,
as is your laugh,
and wide-eyed grin.
Puckered eyebrow when you scowl
in the midst of a musical phrase
as you play your full-bodied bass.

But where he sagged, you expand.
Your heart is your own.

✶ VACATION IN MAINE

Sunlight wakes me in the camper.
Green leaves, white pine limbs
fill each window — a tree house.
Mt. Kathadin's elephantine head
lined with rills of snow — emerges.

The CD plays Wagner's *Die Walküre*.
the opera of incestuous twins
who produce a son, Siegfried.

Sung in German —
I translate for Paul.

Die Walküre continues —
Siegfried has become a man
and looks for adventure —
the way we are now, as
we travel along Maine's winding Route 1.

It takes us to the Alagash
canoed by generations of Cree,
also by Paul, when he was young.
*But nothing has changed
only the trees are taller.*
He shakes his head —

Siegfried has found the sword,
he will slay the dragon —

We stop in the small dank general store —
barrels of sunflower seeds,
mothballs, flour, waxed candles.

(continued)

But nothing has changed—
No dragons here.

The postlude intones and fades—
We move on.

✦ BY THE YANGTZE

No other river's breath smells
so alive or rich as the Yangtze's
flowing past Hankow—
When I close my eyes, my hair, my skin
inhale its wild pungency.
Thirty-five years—
I've come to find her grave.

In summer we played tag on mudflats,
found stones, shells,
and once a human skull!
We dug a hollow for a grave,
fenced it with blue shells, a cross of twigs,
lowered the skull, patted the earth.
My sister sang, my brother and I prayed "Hail Mary."

One winter, for a month
the river spawned an island.
The whole town walked on it;
we played in the golden sand.
One day it sank.

In spring the Yangtze floods,
drowns huts and sometimes children,
its moods a source of fear.
The river matures in autumn.
Tonight, moodiness forgotten,
it bids me welcome.

I never found Mother's grave.
Two officials came to say
"No you cannot go!"
Roads were built
across colonial burial sites.
I bowed. I left.

Drying my tears, I walked
beside the Yangtze's edge,
watching Tai Chi dancers
cleaving the air in silent trance.

✦ THE BRIDGE—AUGUST 19TH, 1948

We steamed under the Golden Gate,
orange girders, latticed webs
the huge bridge peering through fog.
Standing on deck Father pointed
at people walking overhead.
"Children look, America!"

We docked, touched shore,
my legs swayed as I caught my balance
and started walking.

We could drink from
the bathroom faucet,
stared at lions at Fleishhacker Zoo.
Trolleys clanked up and down streets.
No rickshaws.
No beggars.

Years later my daughter drove me
across the Golden Gate.
I saw both sides of
ocean liners coming in,
I was looking down
at the people looking up.

✴ MOUNTAINS

Granite rocks through veils of fog,
greet sedan chair coolies, stopped
to mop their heads and chests,
their rhythmic sing-song lifting us in chairs
on callused shoulders.
My sister and I share one sedan.
Fog clothes and bares
cliffs and streams, as we lurch upward,
to arrive in Kuling for summer.

Holidays in the Lushan range
spelled relief from heat,
and fear of war.
No need to boil water,
or to purify food.
We could swim in rock pools,
gather berries barefoot.

Today, from my home in New Hampshire,
I scan the Franconia Range.
Thin fog obscures valleys, granite rocks,
that promise time to write, sleep
and hike the Profile Trail.
Their outlines through the mist
could be the LuShan Mountains
that followed me across the sea.

✦ SISTER

For Magdalene

I sensed you beside me,
as I walked this morning.
I could hear your breathing
and smell your red brown curls
shot through with gray like mine.
Your delicate hand was on my arm.
You would have been sixty today.
I wanted to tell you about
the children and their lives.

I wanted to pick cattails
as we did the summer before
your car was crumpled
twisting you like metal with it.
I kept the Chinese jade necklace
I took from your desk,
after the funeral.
But I never wear it.

When doing dishes, I sing
German folksongs the way we did.
I hear your humming
with the orioles outside.
Come visit in a dream
so I can see you.

✴ At the Hairdresser

I wait under the drier.
Man erkennt die Frau
an ihrer Frisur,
you recognize a woman
by her hairdo—
my father always said.

The stylist is removing
curlers from the
pink pate of an eighty-year-old.
Her white hair, thin as
dandelion fluff in a breeze, bends
under the beautician's hands.
Nearby a teenager chewing bubblegum,
sits at a mirror watching,
her long brown tresses
gradually redden with dye.

When my body dies
my hair will be the last
to decompose—
its filaments, relics of vanity.

I wait under the drier.

✦ Anarchy at the Tate Gallery in London

The black grand piano is upended,
legs wired over our heads.
Its lid hangs down. Ivory keys dangle
from the fingerboard —
a waterfall of timber slivers.

Croaking music signals change.
Keys are swallowed under the fallboard,
the piano lid moves — silent —
clamps shut.

Three minutes later,
discordant notes whine
through the gallery —
disembowelment
begins again.

God it's all held together
with wires.
Spectators gape —
A small girl points — giggles
How can I practice on that —
I'd have to stand on my head
Older couple, arm in arm,
shake their heads in disbelief —
his brown fedora falls off
as he cranes his neck.

✦ MY FATHER'S COUSIN

When I was a child, Father spoke
of his first cousin
She had auburn ringlets and gypsy eyes.
We were so smitten —
Our families opposed it.

Today, fifty years later,
I sit on her paisley gray couch
as she places her eighty-year-old
diary in my hands.
You must have it. She says
It's about your father.

I squint to make out the faded lines
in that dim light . . .
5/7/1918 —
With a bouquet of fragrant roses
he bid me Auf Wiedersehen at the Bahnhof.

I watch her transparent fingers
tear out the pages, trembling.

✦ Gloves

They were his gloves,
black leather, soft as moss,
wrinkled from use.
Fit my hands perfectly, small hands.
Dad's hands played cello,
stroked my cheek,
held the pen precisely
when drawing graphs.
His gloves, lined with lambswool,
I felt protected
wearing them after he died.

Once I lost one for a day;
found it in my car; balance restored
I stared at my gloved hands at the wheel,
remembering his vanity.
Dad was proud of his dainty surgeon's
hands; dexterous removing
a bullet from a shoulder blade,
tonsils from a child's throat;
making shadow birds on
the playroom walls at bedtime.

"You have my hands," he said.

✦ HANDS

Hand gestures were my world
in my four-language home.
Chinese, from Amah,
German from my parents, English in school.
My parents spoke French
to tell secrets.

My nephew Elliot's hands
longfingered and slender,
are like my mother's hands.
At the piano she easily stretched an octave.
Her palms always smelled like almonds.

Elliot's familiar doctor hands,
mesmerize, waiting to share ideas.
His fingers lie gently folded,
open, accepting. They remind me
of the praying hands of the Dürer painting
on our living room wall in China.

✦ My Brother—My Son

Our mother had already died.
I sat in the sampan
with my arm around Martin.
He was eight, I was twelve—
I mothered him for years.

I call you for dinner, my son,
and use Martin's name.
On the phone as I talk to Martin
I say "Dave."
You are one in my mouth.

Different spirits—
years apart—
Yet out of my throat
comes a name—
Will I always mean one
and speak the other?

✦ IN CHARGE AT ASSISTED LIVING

My stepmother Eva's weak right hand dangles.
Her left moves a brown crucifix
and two white candles in glass holders
to the middle of a card table
draped with white linen,
lays dried flowers around it,
an altar in the center of the lounge.
She moves briskly,
tells me to push chairs in a circle.

Others arrive with walkers,
wheelchairs. We hold hands —
The priest blesses.
In unison we mouth familiar refrains,
pick wafers from a silver box.

Eva smiles, eyes closed.
She has made Sunday Mass
a happening once again.

✴ SAFE HARBOR

for my second husband Paul

Chinese boxcars,
San Francisco trolleys,
Minnesota trains
and New York subways,
brought me, uneasy settler,
to New Hampshire.

You came from
five generations of farmers,
builders, legislators,
born in the valley,
buried with forbears,
in the shade of pines.

Your green Ford truck
on thruway 91
crossed the Connecticut
through woods and farmlands,
took me
to asparagus beds, sugar maples,
a winding road for walking.

The seasons in my life
became predictable, at last.

✦ SUGARING

Paul can't imagine spring
without March sun
pulling sap through tree veins
belling into buckets,
drop after drop of
raw sugar maple fluid.

His forebears sugared.
Syrup aromas invite stories
his grandfather told him
about distilling maple syrup,
as we do today,
one hundred years ago.

His visage softens,
he jokes, reads temperatures,
shyness evaporates with the steam.
As he boils gathered sap,
its fragrant foam roils thickly
into syrup.

Today moist vapor drapes tubs,
tin buckets, iron tongs.
He pours sweet brew into
gallons and pints.
The sticky, smoky liquid
on fingers and tongue,
proof spring has arrived.

✦ FIGS

They open like a flower.
Red-brown, soft on my tongue,
their savory pouch overflowing
with seedy juice — I chew slowly.

My daughter, at the airport
holds out a small basket —
plump, black figs with pink mouths,
I know how you love them.

On a return trip to Europe,
as a child in Italy, I picked green figs
by the Arno River, eating them
unwashed. Mother yelled
They must be cleaned. I went on eating.

I hand a green one to my Yankee husband.
He bites into it, delicate, slowly.
Purses generous lips, smacks them,
waves his tongue over the bite,
eyes roll upward as he grins.
Not bad for a fruit —

✦ Pearls

They warm with wearing,
light, strung together,
rolling next to each other.
When I was a child,
Mother lost the pearl out of her ring:
Pearls are tears, losing one is an omen.
A year later, she died.

I go to the store
to have the clasp secured.
Saleslady, with intake of breath
as I give my name — tells:
He made me try on strand after strand,
to get the right one for his wife.
Long — medium — short choker,
until he chose
the perfect one for you!

I finger my pearls
alive as his love,
against my throat.

✴ ANOTHER LANGUAGE

The stroke hissed into Eva's heart and throat,
chiseled into her brain,
forced her hands askew,
tilted her ankles outward.
I am in a foreign country.
I don't know the language.

I hold her floppy right hand,
her words stumble into German,
Meine Hand ist krank —
My hand is sick.
I answer in English:
It will get better soon, Mother.

Rasping notes escape her throat
as utterance snarls.
I console in German,
in paar Tagen wird's besser,
it will be better in a few days.
I smooth her cheek.

She tries to move her hand once more –
stops — sighs — shakes her head.
Her eyes fill —
I move the red-gold tulips to her bed.
Her eyes widen.
Begins a phrase, in English this time —
my dumb hand . . .

✦ THE ALBINO DEER

Rain-softened twigs, without resistance bowed,
Trailing their weeping leaves, snail-slipping green.
No sounds beat watered face of rocks. A shroud
of greedy mildew reigns, a vulgar queen.
She veils the furrowed bark.
The woodland's dripping rests
as shrinking glade lets pass a cloud-white doe.
Enchanted victim of some demon jest —
white — did forest's arms hold out the day's
warm light, for fear that it might see and brown
your pallid blood — your cradle's warping maze
entombing you, preserve your snowy crown?
Each chained to each, from nature's grace exiled,
together mourn the forest and its child.

✴ THREE-HUNDRED-YEAR-OLD SUGAR MAPLE

Its wizened presence haunts my daily walk.
Deep fissures in the bark breathe, as morning spreads —
The sky peers through branches —

I hear the tree talk to me.
It tells of horses pulling scoots or sleds
in the snow, filled with sap buckets —

of women in long skirts
tapping wooden spouts in its sides
so sap could flow —

of strong men piling wood
to feed the roaring fire
boiling sap into maple syrup.

It tells of the hurricane of '38
that wrestled with its branches,
and amputated half its side.

The fluid bulge of a limb,
like a weal-scarred arm,
beckons as if to wrap around me.

Leaves hang in drapes, high
over the familiar divided trunk, open
almost to its roots — alive — alive.

✦ THE LINDBERGH CRATE, CANAAN, MAINE

For Gray Jacobik

Inside the crate
in which the *Spirit of St Louis*
was ferried in 1928, from Marseilles
to New York Harbor, on the *Memphis*,
Larry Ross, ponytail wet from the shower,
talks nonstop — gestures
at the newly painted ceiling.

Bought and fixed it for $3,000.
He hammers a rusted joist
bulging from uneven floor planks,
adjusts a corner portrait
on the English spruce walls.
That's Lindbergh when he was sixteen.

He stretches, grins.
*Admiral Burrage, friend of Lindbergh's,
captain of the* Memphis,
*made a guest cabin out of it.
When he returned to the U.S.A.,
he shipped it to Contoocook, N.H.,
his summer home.*

His eyes glow, he leaps up.
straightens a bronze bust of Lindbergh.
*After his death, the cabin rotted.
I saw it advertised for sale —
picked it up in a flatbed truck —
that was in 1990.*

*On Charles Lindbergh Day every June
we have a kid's festival of planes and rides.*

I've felt connected to
Charles Lindbergh since I was a kid.
He had a dream,
made it happen. Lived it.

We left Ross living
in his dream—
All morning the glow filled our car.

✴ LILACS

The wild scent precedes clumps of blossoms,
gently swaying between old trees.
The moss-scarred cellar hole hides
the roots of the annual riot
of violet, white and torrid purple.
I begin my yearly ritual
of selecting, cutting, pruning,
hiding my face in perfumed clusters.

Someone, long since gone,
tilled the disappearing acres,
carefully planted these lilacs,
loved, raised children and moved on;
leaving a legacy of blooms,
year after year after year.

Did they know that generations later,
their flowering sprays
would crown my table,
enter my kitchen
with abundant fragrance,
leave tiny petals on my floor?

✦ DAFFODILS

They arrived wet in a FedEx box,
sent by my daughter.
Three dozen daffodils in the
midst of an April snowstorm.

Her card said "Happy Spring."
Unpredictable as a mountain rill
splashing through my life,
her moods like eddies spin around me.

The flowers shoot rays onto my table.
Each blossom's heart-shaped
saffron petals cup an
egg-yolk trumpet perfectly.

I will see her next month.
Like yellow stars
the flowers weave and nod this morning.
Promise of a sunny visit.

✶ PENUMBRA

Snake Hill, Wuchang, China,
autumn of 1940.
I stand holding father's hand.
As the sun darkens around us, Chinese climbers
beat drums.
All point to the sky.
An evil omen. The war will continue.

Today, in my home by our New Hampshire pond,
I watch the moon enter the sun's perimeter.
Slower than a sunset the eclipse begins.
The living room's cold
Christmas tree lights are out.
Unwrapped gifts, books,
red pajamas, yellow socks
sit in a growing artificial dusk.

As the moon covers the sun's face,
I put a blanket around my shoulders.
I want Dad to be alive —
Shadows deepen —
I feel light filling my bones.

✦ STAIRS—WUHAN

How often I ran up and down these steps
my braids bouncing against my back,
my hands trailing the banister,
my life overflowing like the streets outside,
vendors stirring aromatic treats,
noisy gambling by mahjong players,
the Yangtze's odor seeping over all,
my mother still alive.

Now coming home after fifty years,
I stand in our old apartment building,
before the rusted elevator gates,
peering up at five floors
ending in the sky.
The lift stands, as it did
the morning she jumped.
But it is motionless, unused, barred off.
In a circle around the shaft, the stairs
reach up, shelves of cupped cement,
familiar as the knuckles of my hand.

Everything has changed,
nothing has changed.
I am older than Mother
when she died.
Today I turn around to climb the stairs,
my feet fit in the grooves
like easy shoes—
knowing where they lead.

✴ Painting my Rocking Chair

Sunlight envelops the porch.
I set the creaky, 43-year-old rocker
on the table and slosh on red-brown paint.
Green when my aunt gave it to me
after I had my daughter in our
New York City apartment.

I remember my two-year-old Krista
sitting on the kitchen floor,
playing with coffee pot innards
I'd pick her up and swing on the swaying rocker.
"My chair" she'd say.

It moved with us
into the White Mountains.
For years it sat on the porch through ice
and snow, its paint chipped —
as my marriage folded.

I took it with me to my new
husband's home in the woods.
Today the chair and I both need paint.
After the paint dries,
I will sit on my chair and rock!

✦ REQUIEM

The first time I returned,
thirty years later,
they said the cemetery
had disappeared,
the grave site was lost,
my query unanswered.

Twenty years later, I went again.
Steaming noodle stands, bartering flower vendors,
circled a hospital
built on top of the cemetery grounds.
In the cobblestone courtyard,
I looked for relics of granite headstones.
I waited for rising tears
but only felt the gentle spring rain.

My mother, the doctor,
would lie there in peace.

✦ IRONING

As the quiet rain splatters the window,
I iron in the kitchen, lifting
one piece after another from the blue basket.
When I press the crimson tablecloth
I bought from the Amish farm store, years ago,
the smell of damp cotton rises—

It makes me think of the Chinese laundry woman
when I was a child, who sang
while ironing my father's white shirts—
her black hair coiled in a fragrant bun,
a bee humming monotone
enveloped in wet smoke—

My first husband
wore white shirts as well.
I ironed them while he shaved,
pale with anticipation,
for his evening's concert.

But no shirts to iron now.
The creases in my linen skirt evaporate—
Flowery pillowcases billow as I steam,
as if all the pressings of my life
floated around this room.

I finish with a chiffon shawl,
the color of sunrise, to wear
to my daughter's wedding.

✦ NINETIETH BIRTHDAY PARTY

Pressed in her recliner,
she tries to smile as she recognizes me.
I pin her corsage of tiny pink roses
to her navy blouse as her breath comes in soft gasps.

We stand around her at the table
festive with a chocolate cake crowned
by three chocolate violins and a pink number ninety.
My nephew makes a speech
about Mother Eva's ability to parent her stepchildren.
I say a word about her courage, as I cry.

My brother sings an old Russian song
taught him by our Russian dentist when he was a boy.
We all sing "Happy Birthday."
Children, grandchildren,
and four great-grandchildren fight to blow out candles.

She mumbles, *"I want to live to be a hundred"*
and grins.

This is the week before she dies.

✦ COMPLETION

for my father

We arrived in America fifty-two years
ago today, I begin.
Missionary elders crowd the hall.
My name is unfamiliar
but we share China childhoods
a time before world wars—
when women's feet were hobbled,
and streets still lined with beggars.
I read a poem about the Yangtze.

We talk of nannies with braided hair
spinners of magic turtle legends.
Aromas almost rise at tales
of sesame fried dough, steamed noodles,
sugar cane and green pickled eggs.
Swimming in rock pools melds
with ascents to mountains in sedan chairs.
"Has China changed?"

He saved my mother's life
from Typhoid—
the white-haired man speaks
of my doctor father.
He delivered my uncle into this world,
a woman in a walker whispers.
He imported German Attabrin
to cure my malaria,
yells another, rises and claps—
on a golden summer afternoon
in Minnesota.

✦ CHINA REUNION AFTER FIFTY YEARS

Fluorescent lights clear the floors
of the church dormitory
as we pile nighties, shoes, on
bunk beds with green wool blankets.
School was American School, Kikung-Shan
Rooster Head Mountain in China.

In that last year we took the train,
fleeing attacks from the Red Chinese army.
Snuggled by twos in train berths
we heard shots in the distance.
I was fourteen.

Later, in Hongkong,
we lived in an old school for the blind,
studied in rooms overlooking the ocean,
like siblings—good days and bad.
War was behind us.

I see Nick today, same twisted grin,
a few wrinkles, bragging, as usual,
sweeping graying hair out of his face
with a well remembered move.
Joking, exaggerating, funny.

Lois and I share work plans—
"I'm not ready to retire."
We gossip about Ruthie and her
daughter's son in Baghdad .

Suddenly a bell clangs on a glass—
Dave begins an old hymn,
"Praise God from whom all blessings flow."
Like summer evenings in the mountains
when we all sang—and listened to the echoes.

✶ CHANCE STOP AT STEARNS POINT ROAD

I asked the tour bus driver to stop,
got out to take pictures
of the familiar willow
brushing the roof, and the wicker chair
on the tilted porch floor.
In my mind I see my kids climbing the apple tree,
playing hide and seek in the backyard.
The screens are gone — the paint is chipped —
swallows play *chase me* as they always did.

Thirty-two years, since we bought
that three-room vacation house on Shelter Island,
perfect with its dirt road, trimmed hedges,
a haven from Manhattan's traffic lights.
Friday nights, sleeping kids in back, we drove
there and listened to the chatting frogs,
the shrill sea gull's call.

I nursed our son on our screen porch.
At Easter apple blossoms bloomed —
At Thanksgiving the beach was white with frost,
laughter, children's voices.

✴ LEGACY FOR KRISTA

9/21/02

For your marriage
I give you two Chinese scrolls.
Paired gray Mandarin ducks,
necks curved, striped black wings,
resting among reeds on soft sand,
as they caress each other's feathers —
black brush strokes of Chinese calligraphy
quotes lines from poet Chuo Weng
Cool moon with a clear breeze
over waterside North . . .

Mandarin ducks in China
symbols of caretaking in marriage.

Grandpa gave the paintings
to your dad and me
years ago, as a wedding gift.
They've hung in my study
since your father's death.

Today Dad's cello music
rises through the mist
above the ducks' wings —
near their webbed feet
is my childhood in Hankow

✦ PEN'S BRIDGE

Paul and Pen built model bridges
first on ping-pong tables,
later over ditches and streams.
Twenty years older,
Pen was his younger brother's guide
into the grown-up world.

After Pen's death,
Paul built a bridge of pine
across the stream behind our house.
How strange that its delicate arc
brought back my China childhood,
summers in Kuling picking lotus pods,
standing on bridges over mountain pools.
I lost a sister, I know how memories console.

Today, our anniversary, I walk to the bridge,
stop on its swaying center, and meet Paul.
New England balsam, dark green moss of banks
surround us, weaving a web of comfort.
Are lotus blossoms floating underneath?

✦ Notes on the Illustrations

COVER: A Chinese bridge spans the maps of two continents, Asia and North America. The red dot on the map of China represents the beginning of the author's story while the red dot on the coast of California represents the continuation of her life in America. The red line down the middle divides the story into two parts while the bridge arching over time and space combines the two life experiences.

Pages following the section title pages:

I.   China is represented by a peony. A stylized bridge moves through the flower and emerges on the other side.

II. A person holding an umbrella walks through a surrealistic space on the top of a bridge. The umbrella provides a spot of color and a small simulacrum of comfort and safety.

III. The Golden Gate Bridge is the welcoming path into a new world.

IV. The covered bridge, surrounded by nature, reflects the simplicity and solidity of life in New Hampshire.

V.   Pen's bridge echoes the first image of the series which is of a bridge moving through a flower representing China. Here we have a bridge moving in front of a maple leaf which is a metaphor for the continuation of the poet's life in New England.

✦ About the Author

DOROTHY B. ANDERSON was born in Marburg, Germany, and went to China as an infant during the Nazi era. Her parents were physicians of German-Jewish background. They lived in Wuhan, China during the Japanese occupation. Her mother died there. Dorothy and her family came to America in 1948. She lived in Franconia, New Hampshire for 15 years and was on the board of directors of the Frost Place. She is a family therapist, is married to a tree farmer, and has two grown children.

✦ About the Illustrator

DONNA BRUHL has a degree in art and history from the University of Minnesota. She has also studied at the Minneapolis School of Art and Design, The Penland School of Arts and Crafts and the Cambridge College of Art in Cambridge, England. For the last thirty years, she has made and exhibited functional stoneware and porcelain pottery. She is currently involved in the production of large-scale sculpture and tiles. Illustrating this book has enabled her to explore the use of cut paper in the creation of graphic design, a newfound sensibility she intends to incorporate into her other art.

What We Will Give Each Other
by Sidney Hall Jr.
"These poems are disciplined, clear-eyed and clear-headed
like their Greek, Latin and Chinese forebears. Sidney Hall
achieves a kind of sophisticated simplicity that is rare among his
contemporaries. Call him a neoclassicist seasoned by the spirits of
Zen and Taoism—his poems are revelations, beautiful and true."
—Sam Hamill

ISBN 0-9636413-0-1 / 64 pp.
Paper / $9.95

Viewpoint
by Juli Nunlist
"Slender is a word sometimes used to compliment a woman's figure;
but we never use the word to compliment a woman's poems. Yet it
is the right word for Juli Nunlist's elegant and moving poems: for
they are slender the way a Renaissance dagger is, or the high, perfect
notes of a countertenor's voice. Such beauty of illumined slenderness
can come only at the end of a long, complicated, and almost always
dark apprenticeship in the art; indeed, it is always a hard-won
beauty. Gratitude is the truest response to Juli Nunlist's poems."
— Don Sheehan, Director (retired)
The Frost Place, Franconia, NH

ISBN 0-9760896-3-7 / 120 pp.
Paper / $14.95

Crossing Points
by Anne R.P. Dewees
A journal in poetry of an unforgettable safari trip through
Tanzania, including Serengeti National Park, the Ngorongoro
Conservation Area, and the Arusha National Park. This handsome
chapbook is printed on fine papers with colored endpapers.

ISBN 0-9760896-1-0 /40 pp.
Chapbook / $8.95